A Season of Gratitude

Wanda Strange

Publisher: bylisabell
Radical Women (DBA)
PO Box 782
Granbury, TX 76048
www.bylisabell.com

ISBN-10: 0-9983308-5X
ISBN-13: 978-0-9983308-5-3

DEDICATION

To Cindi Bedell, who encouraged me to develop the habit of journaling my thoughts of gratitude.

Be careful for nothing; but in everything by prayer and supplication with thanksgiving let your requests be made known unto God. And the peace of God, which passeth all understanding, shall keep your hearts and minds through Christ Jesus.

Philippians 4: 6-7 KJV

ACKNOWLEDGMENTS

LISA BELL – CHEERLEADER, ENCOURAGER, PATIENT TEACHER – MY SISTER

BEVERLY WARD – PROOF READER, EDITOR, ENCOURAGER, PRAYER WARRIOR – MY FRIEND

The expectation that we can be immersed in suffering and loss daily and not be touched by it is as unrealistic as expecting to be able to walk through water without getting wet.
Rachel Naomi Remen

Gratitude:
My Ultimate Coping Mechanism

A small group of physically and emotionally exhausted colleagues gathered in the conference room. Every oncology nurse identifies with the grief and pain of losing patients. Often the notification of one death followed closely by another compounds and complicates the grieving process. Failure to acknowledge multiple losses increases vulnerability.

After the loss of several beloved patients, the group identified symptoms of compassion fatigue and burnout. Realizing our inability to utilize appropriate coping skills and address an overwhelming burden led us to seek guidance.

Over the course of several weeks, a professional counselor facilitated the group in identifying needs, team building, and developing healthy coping mechanisms.

The suggestion to journal met opposition from the group. "I've journaled from time to time," offered one of the participants. "However, I found myself guarding my written thoughts. I was afraid I might die before I got the chance to burn it."

We chuckled, breaking the tension, but identified with her candid confession.

The facilitator instructed the group, "Your assignment this week is to journal daily. Write down your frustrations, anger, and pain. All of it – the good – the bad – the ugly. Once you've gotten it all out on paper, write ten things for which you are grateful."

Though I view life from the perspective of an oncology nurse, I realize compassion fatigue, burnout, and life's challenges are not limited to the medical profession. We live in a stressful, anxiety-producing world. The news media reports tragedies and strife daily. The crises get personal: layoffs – divorce – health concerns – accidents – caregiver stress – grief and loss – chronic pain – finances – fractured relationships – on and on.

I took the assignment seriously and chose to embrace gratitude. The more I viewed life through a lens of thanksgiving, the more grateful I felt. My journey began, and the practice of journaling my thoughts of gratitude became my primary coping mechanism.

My precious friend and colleague presented us with a special gift that Christmas

– a five-year gratitude journal. Each day I journal one thought. As I record joyous little moments, I focus on the positive. Reading the previous entries, I recall delightful people, places and times. Even on my worst days – through life's most challenging circumstances - I find something for which to be grateful.

Researchers indicate it takes thirty days to form a habit. As I share my personal Season of Gratitude, I hope you join me on a rewarding journey and develop the practice of expressing thanksgiving for life's blessings.

There is something about gratitude that has a way of multiplying our sense of resources. It is the secret of creative coping. Of all the options we have, it is perhaps the most creative and the most gracious of all.

John Claypool

Love LIFE *Family* **Friends**

SUNSETS   *A*   *Butterflies*

𝔑𝔦𝔤𝔥𝔱 𝔖𝔨𝔦𝔢𝔰   *Season*   Sunshine

ℜ𝔞𝔦𝔫𝔟𝔬𝔴𝔰   *of*   **Joy**

Health   Music

Books   *Gratitude*   𝒜rt

New Beginnings   *New Life*

𝔖𝔲𝔪𝔪𝔢𝔯 𝔙𝔞𝔦𝔫   *Flowers*

Food   **Shelter**   Provision

𝔖𝔞𝔩𝔳𝔞𝔱𝔦𝔬𝔫

SIGHT – HEARING – TASTE – FEEL - SMELLS

Season of Gratitude
Day One

The dictionary defines gratitude as the quality of being thankful, readiness to show appreciation for and return kindness.

For me, November begins a season of thanksgiving – an opportunity to focus on life's many blessings. I resolve to express gratitude and show kindness.

I begin day one of this season with gratitude for life. I woke up this morning, blessed with another day. The sun shines brightly. Three mighty oaks stand strong in my backyard. Nature reminds me of God's loving care and faithfulness.

It is of the LORD's mercies that we are not consumed, because his compassions fail not. They are new every morning: great is thy faithfulness.

Lamentations 3: 22-23 KJV

_____

_____

_____

_____

_____

_____

_____

_____

_____

_____

_____

_____

_____

_____

_____

_____

_____

_____

Season of Gratitude
Day Two

The Bible on the desk in my entryway lies open to one of my favorite scripture passages. I gratefully acknowledge that in each stage of my life, regardless of circumstances, God has a plan and a grand design for my life.

He promises to be found. However, His promise requires me to do my part. I must continually seek Him. I excitedly anticipate the plan He has for me today and through each season of my life.

For I know the thoughts that I think toward you, saith the LORD, thoughts of peace, and not of evil, to give you an expected end. Then shall ye call upon me, and ye shall go and pray unto me, and I will hearken unto you. And ye shall seek me, and find me, when ye shall search for me with all your heart.

Jeremiah 29:11-13 KJV

A Season of Gratitude

Season of Gratitude
Day Three

Today I am thankful for and celebrate life's little moments. Yesterday I captured a photo of a beautiful monarch butterfly. This morning I woke to refreshing rain and cooler temperatures. A red bird busily hops from one spot to another, entertaining me as I linger over a cup of coffee.

Jesus assured us that He came to give us an abundantly full life. Too often, I rush from one activity to another and fail to show adequate appreciation for the artistry of nature.

I remind myself to slow down, pause for a few moments, and sincerely appreciate all the beauty surrounding me.

The earth is the LORD's, and the fullness thereof; the world, and they that dwell therein.
Psalm 24:1 KJV

_____

_____

_____

_____

_____

_____

_____

_____

_____

_____

_____

_____

_____

_____

_____

_____

_____

_____

_____

_____

_____

Season of Gratitude
Day 4

The summer of 2017, my husband, Kerry, and I celebrated our forty-eighth wedding anniversary. My husband balances my craziness and keeps me grounded. He supports and encourages me to be the best I can be. As teenagers, we had no idea what challenges awaited us. The difficult times bonded us and strengthened our relationship.

I am thankful for our many memories - for the good times as well as the hard ones. I value my prudent spouse as a special gift from the Lord.

House and riches are the inheritance of fathers: and a prudent wife is from the Lord.
Proverbs 19:14 KJV

_____

_____

_____

_____

_____

_____

_____

_____

_____

_____

_____

_____

_____

_____

_____

_____

_____

_____

_____

Season of Gratitude
Day 5

God blessed me with an amazing daughter. As much as anyone I've ever known, Ginger shows patience, perseverance, and tenacity. She exhibits characteristics of honesty and loyalty. She continues to challenge me to develop these traits in my own life. Her love and friendship enriches my life every day.

I thank God for choosing me to be her mother.

Lo, children are an heritage of the LORD: and the fruit of the womb is his reward.
Psalm 127:3 KJV

Season of Gratitude
Day 6

I share history with my siblings. They understand my quirks without explanation. They get my weirdness, my oddities, and love me unconditionally.

I am grateful for the bond we share. I love my sisters and my brother.

Be kindly affected one to another with brotherly love; in honour preferring one another.
Romans 12:10 KJV

_____

_____

_____

_____

_____

_____

_____

_____

_____

_____

_____

_____

_____

_____

_____

_____

Season of Gratitude
Day 7

The magnificent oak trees in our backyard remind me to celebrate deep roots: ancestral roots, the roots of strong lasting friendships, but most of all being rooted and grounded in my faith.

Because of their roots, the oaks withstand winds and storms and continue to stand strong. A deep, abiding faith does the same in storms of life.

Jesus warned, *in this world we will have trouble.*

Our hope remains in Him. Take heart - He is in control and has overcome the world.

Thank you, Lord. You are in charge. I am not - and don't want or need to be.

And he shall be like a tree planted by the rivers of water, that bringeth forth his fruit in his season; his leaf also shall not wither; and whatsoever he doeth shall prosper.
Psalm 1:3 KJV

Season of Gratitude
Day 8

Despite the divisive, chaotic, mean-spirited nature of politics and politicians, I gratefully celebrate the sacrifice of the men and women who guaranteed our freedoms and our right to choose leadership. I seriously consider my civic responsibility to vote.

With all our nation's faults and problems, I gratefully claim the birthright of American citizenship. I remind myself regularly - no matter who occupies the White House, God is in control and Jesus Christ is Lord and King.

And Jesus answering said unto them, Render to Caesar the things that are Caesar's, and to God the things that are God's. And they marveled at him.
Mark 12:17 KJV

Season of Gratitude
Day 9

Today I traveled to Dallas for my mammogram. It marked the first screening mammogram since my breast cancer diagnosis. After five years, I graduated from diagnostic to screening. My gratitude is multi-layered. I am thankful for life as a cancer survivor/thriver. I am grateful for my amazing medical team.

Since I'm no longer required to see them medically, perhaps I should make a social visit.

Heal me, O Lord, and I shall be healed; save me, and I shall be saved: for thou art my praise.
Jeremiah 17:14 KJV

_____

_____

_____

_____

_____

_____

_____

_____

_____

_____

_____

_____

_____

_____

_____

_____

_____

_____

Season of Gratitude
Day 10

I consistently seek to make my home a place of peace. I desire all who enter to find my home a warm and welcoming place. During construction, we wrote on the foundation and the framework. Choosing our favorite scriptures, we chose to incorporate our faith and make Christ the foundation of our home.

What makes a house a home? Certainly not structure or furnishings – even the most elegantly decorated house may feel cold and foreboding. Home should offer comfort for each family member.

I thank God for giving us our home – more than I dreamed – more than I imagined – more than I deserved.

Come see me anytime. You're always welcome.

Be not forgetful to entertain strangers: for thereby some have entertained angels unawares.
Hebrews 13:2 KJV

Season of Gratitude
Day 11

Observed annually on November 11th, Veteran's Day honors those who served in the military. I reflect on the debt I owe to so many. Because of veterans who willingly enlisted, I enjoy freedom.

What a privilege to participate as Bluff Dale ISD honors the veterans in our community; one of the many reasons I love Bluff Dale. How special to see all the photos celebrating veterans who secured our rights.

To the veterans and to active service members and their families – thank you for your sacrificial service.

Greater love hath no man than this, that a man lay down his life for his friends.
John 15:13 KJV

Season of Gratitude
Day 12

Each day my gratitude journal begins with a quote or scripture to stimulate a thought followed by space to record my personal reflections.

Today's quote from Andrew Murray, "Answered prayer is the interchange of love between the Father and His child."

My 2014 entry, " I am thankful for answered prayers, even when it isn't the answer I was looking for - even when the answer is no."

How can I be thankful for the challenges of life?

Though difficult to appreciate when walking through the hard times, the worst experiences of my life shaped me into the woman I am. While I can't always say, "Thank you, Lord, for trouble." I am thankful God uses the bad times to grow my faith and uses everything for good.

My Father sees the big picture and is molding me. God promises to provide strength for each challenge.

But they that wait upon the LORD shall renew their strength; they shall mount up with wings as eagles; they shall run, and not be weary; and they shall walk, and not faint. Isaiah 40:31 KJV

Some days my heart soars and my soul sings. Other days God blesses me with energy and strength to run through the activities of my life. Most of all, on the hardest days, I praise God for the grace to walk – to simply put one foot in front of the other.

And we know that all things work together for good to them that love God, to them who are the called according to his purpose.

Romans 8:28 KJV

Season of Gratitude
Day 13

Music speaks to my soul. As I observe the super moon, I recall a beautiful Psalm that inspired Tom Fetke's anthem, *The Majesty and Glory of Your Name*. Music expresses emotions and leads me into worship.

I marvel that the God who created the night sky is mindful of me.

Tonight I am thankful for God's magnificent creation and for music as an expression of my praise.

O LORD, our Lord, how excellent is thy name in all the earth! who hast set thy glory above the heavens. Out of the mouth of babes and sucklings hast thou ordained strength because of thine enemies, that thou mightest still the enemy and the avenger. When I consider thy heavens, the work of thy fingers, the moon and the stars, which thou hast ordained;

What is man, that thou art mindful of him? and the son of man, that thou visitest him?

For thou hast made him a little lower than the angels, and hast crowned him with glory and honour. Thou madest him to have dominion over the works of thy hands; thou hast put all things under his feet: All sheep and oxen, yea, and the beasts of the field; The fowl of the air, and the fish of the sea, and whatsoever passeth through the paths of the seas.

O LORD our Lord, how excellent is thy name in all the earth!

Psalm 8 KJV

Season of Gratitude
Day 14

My amazingly talented and loving nieces and nephews, their spouses, great nieces and nephews add so much to my life.

We share a unique relationship. I marvel at their accomplishments and watch with pride as they parent precious children.

Though geography separates us, love binds us together. I cherish the memories of good times we share.

All nieces are brilliant and beautiful... and obviously take after their aunt.
Author Unknown

_____

_____

_____

_____

_____

_____

_____

_____

_____

_____

_____

_____

_____

_____

_____

_____

_____

Season of Gratitude
Day 15

Even through the darkness and pain –
even when life is hard, I choose to trust and
praise Him.

Because we live in a broken world, we
suffer pain. Every day I encounter someone
who experiences pain, suffering, and
questioning.

As I reflect on a lifetime of challenges, I
am grateful for the way God carried me
through the hard times. He surrounded me
with amazing, supportive friends, for which I
am eternally grateful. He commands us to
support each other through struggles.

Serving and supporting others provides a
God given purpose that gives meaning to life.

*These things I have spoken unto
you, that in me ye might have
peace. In the world ye shall have
tribulation: but be of good cheer;
I have overcome the world.*
John 16:33 KJV

A Season of Gratitude

_____

_____

_____

_____

_____

_____

_____

_____

_____

_____

_____

_____

_____

_____

_____

_____

_____

Season of Gratitude
Day 16

The patients and colleagues who left fingerprints on my heart continue to inspire me. I am grateful for the career that afforded me the opportunity to pursue my passion and my calling.

As I enter the retirement phase of my life, I carry memories of special people in my heart – an integral part of me. Continued relationships bless and enrich my life.

Our fingerprints don't fade from the lives we touch.
Judy Blume

_____

_____

_____

_____

_____

_____

_____

_____

_____

_____

_____

_____

_____

_____

_____

_____

Season of Gratitude
Day 17

I treasure each friend who blesses and enriches my life. Over the years these precious companions walked with me through good times as well as difficult circumstances.

Because of a shared history, they understand my weird quirks. Even though distance separates us, our sweet memories bond us together.

God continues to bring new friends into my life. As we journey through this world, our love and support of each other makes us stronger.

The best kind of friend is the one you could sit on a porch with, never saying a word, and walk away feeling like that was the best conversation you've had.
Author Unknown

A friend loveth at all times, and a brother is born for adversity.
Proverbs 17:17 KJV

_____

_____

_____

_____

_____

_____

_____

_____

_____

_____

_____

_____

_____

_____

_____

_____

_____

_____

Season of Gratitude
Day 18

When I married Kerry Strange, I gained an incredible extended family. The godly matriarch of the Cargile family instilled these values in her children. The young, pregnant widow of a tenant farmer, Odessa, faced unimaginably difficult circumstances. While the nation faced the Great Depression of the 1930's, she confronted the challenge of raising seven children. She left the farm, rented a large house, and opened a boarding house in Commerce, Texas.

What a legacy she left! She encouraged her children with positive words, both spoken and written. Throughout her life she modeled faith and kindness, and showed us how to age gracefully. I thank God for each member of this incredible clan and their continued influence on my life. Odessa's legacy continues from generation to generation.

Her children arise up, and call her blessed; her husband also, and he praiseth her.
Proverbs 31:28 KJV

_____

_____

_____

_____

_____

_____

_____

_____

_____

_____

_____

_____

_____

_____

_____

_____

Season of Gratitude
Day 19

I am grateful for and depend on the love, support, and prayers of my family of faith.

During the most difficult challenges, we lift each other up. When I can't pray for myself, I count on my brothers and sisters in Christ to intercede for me. When I am strong, I intercede for them. I love my local church as well as my family of faith around the world.

No matter where we worship, we share a bond of Christian love.

Not forsaking the assembling of ourselves together, as the manner of some is; but exhorting one another: and so much the more, as ye see the day approaching.
Hebrews 10:25 KJV

Season of Gratitude
Day 20

Even when I can't see God's plan, I trust Him to work for my good. God's faithfulness endures. He views my life from an eternal perspective. Jeremiah 29:31 assures me that He knows his plan for me.

I often fail to understand and sometimes find it hard to pray. During those times faithful warriors pray for me. The Holy Spirit hears my pain and my deepest longing. When I don't know the words to say, the Holy Spirit intercedes for me.

Likewise the Spirit also helpeth our infirmities: for we know not what we should pray for as we ought: but the Spirit itself maketh intercession for us with groanings which cannot be uttered.

Romans 8:26 KJV

_____

_____

_____

_____

_____

_____

_____

_____

_____

_____

_____

_____

_____

_____

_____

_____

Season of Gratitude
Day 21

The chill in the air and the changing color of the trees promise a change in the season. The unseasonably warm weather in Texas this year delayed seasonal color.

Today I express gratitude for the rhythm of nature.

To everything there is a season, and a time to every purpose under the heaven.
Ecclesiastes 3:1 KJV

_____

_____

_____

_____

_____

_____

_____

_____

_____

_____

_____

_____

_____

_____

_____

_____

_____

Season of Gratitude
Day 22

It's too warm for a fire, so I light candles. I am grateful for my home and hearth.

As the warm glow of the candles illuminates the room, I reflect on Christ – the Light of the World. He commanded us, his followers, to share that light – to serve each other.

I praise God for quiet, still, unhurried moments.

Neither do men light a candle, and put it under a bushel, but on a candlestick; and it giveth light unto all that are in the house.
Matthew 5:15 KJV

_____

_____

_____

_____

_____

_____

_____

_____

_____

_____

_____

_____

_____

_____

_____

_____

Season of Gratitude
Day 23

I love the smell of traditional Thanksgiving foods cooking in the house. Holiday scents add to the festive feeling of any room. Instead of cooking today, I fill the room with the scents from wax melts and candles to stimulate my nostalgic senses.

Today, a rose, likely the last of the season, captured my attention.

God made us and all creation – fearfully and wonderfully. Our senses allow us to fully appreciate God's creation. I am grateful for the sweet smells of food in the oven, spices, flowers, rain, a fireplace, fresh brewed coffee, and so much more. I celebrate the ability to see the beauty of the earth – to hear nature's symphony – to touch and feel an embrace, to taste amazing foods – all especially appreciated during this time of year.

I will praise thee; for I am fearfully and wonderfully made: marvellous are thy works; and that my soul knoweth right well.
Psalm 139:14 KJV

_____

_____

_____

_____

_____

_____

_____

_____

_____

_____

_____

_____

_____

_____

_____

_____

Season of Gratitude
Day 24

One of our Thanksgiving traditions involves the ritual of sharing one special blessing of the current year. I am particularly grateful for family time. I never take for granted any time we gather as a family. One phone call, an accident, or illness quickly changes everything.

By God's grace we sit down to a table filled with an abundance of good food – in a warm home to shelter us from the elements – with people who love each other.

How could I ask for more?

O Lord, thou art my God; I will exalt thee, I will praise thy name; for thou hast done wonderful things; thy counsels of old are faithfulness and truth.
Isaiah 25:1 KJV

_____

_____

_____

_____

_____

_____

_____

_____

_____

_____

_____

_____

_____

_____

_____

Season of Gratitude
Day 25

As I turn the page on Thanksgiving and prepare for Advent, I pray for peace. Acutely aware of the discord in our nation, in our world, and in far too many homes, I gratefully acknowledge God's gift of peace.

Too often, I get wrapped up in the mess of life and fail to experience the peace Christ brings to my heart in the good times and bad.

I offer this prayer in the days following thanksgiving.

Intervene, Lord, bring peace where there is strife, and calm where there is chaos. Help me to listen to Your voice and be an instrument of Your peace. As I prepare my heart for Christmas, help me be still and acknowledge You as Lord of my life and Prince of Peace.

The Prayer of St. Francis of Assisi

Lord, make us instruments of your
peace.
Where there is hatred, let us sow
love;
Where there is injury, pardon;
Where there is discord, union;
Where there is doubt, faith;
Where there is despair, hope;
Where there is darkness, light;
Where there is sadness, joy;
O Divine Master, Grant that we
may not so much seek
To be consoled as to console,
To be understood as to understand,
To be loved as to love.
For it is in giving that we receive;
It is in pardoning that we are
pardoned;
And it is in dying that we are
born to eternal life.
Amen.

Season of Gratitude
Day 26

A colorful prism hangs in my kitchen where I observe it every day. A special gift from a treasured friend reminds me to disseminate light.

The dictionary defines a prism as a solid body used to disperse light into a spectrum or to reflect rays of light.

I am grateful for the many people in my life who serve as prisms reflecting God's light and love.

That ye may be blameless and harmless, the sons of God, without rebuke, in the midst of a crooked and perverse nation, among whom ye shine as lights in the world;

Philippians 2:15 KJV

Season of Gratitude
Day 27

On the first Sunday of Advent, we light the candle of hope. More than wishing or dreaming for a desired result, hope expects action. We believe with certainty the Bible is true and confidently anticipate God to fulfill His promises.

While November allows us to focus on gratitude, Advent prepares our spirits for Christmas.

Traditionally, I spend the weekend following Thanksgiving decorating my home for Christmas. Each year I rearrange and remove items to make room for Christmas decorations.

In much the same way, I must rearrange my schedule and my priorities to make room for Jesus in my heart and life. God meets me when I clear space for Him.

My Advent prayer – Come Lord Jesus. My hope is in You. There is room in my heart for You.

And she brought forth her firstborn son, and wrapped him in swaddling clothes, and laid him in a manger; because there was no room for them in the inn.
Luke 2:7 KJV

Season of Gratitude
Day 28

An online Bible study, *Because of Bethlehem* (*Max Lucado's Advent study*), challenged me to look for light this week. Today the sun shone brilliantly and disseminated rays of light across the sky.

Daily responsibilities often preoccupy my thoughts, and I inadequately appreciate the beauty before me.

I enthusiastically accepted the assignment and intentionally explored a spectacular mid-day display of God's masterpiece.

I didn't have to look far to find light - simply open my eyes to the wonderful creation around me. Thank you, Lord

Note: The cover photo for *A Season of Gratitude* resulted from this fall adventure.

The heavens declare the glory of God; and the firmament sheweth his handywork.
Psalm 19:1 KJV

Season of Gratitude
Day 29

I never expected to live in a small town. However, God planned something awesome for my autumn years.

When we visited the Mountain Lakes property, the beauty of the land compelled us to look deeper. "It's not that far from the city. There's a lot to do in Granbury. Stephenville's a college town. I'll be okay. It's way better than some of the desolate places Kerry's shown me recently." I rationalized as we made a decision to buy land away from our suburban, DeSoto home.

My concerns about being bored proved unfounded. Church, sewing circle, Bible study, book club, garden and study club, exercise classes, ice cream socials, hamburger suppers, fish fries - only problem is finding time to work it all in.

The spectacular views drew us here - the community provided the connection we needed to feel at home.

We found a priceless treasure – Bluff Dale, Texas – an eclectic community of amazingly loving individuals. Genuine people, who sincerely care for each other, celebrate

A Season of Gratitude

good times and walk together through the difficult ones.

I love this place and the people I proudly call my neighbors and my friends. I truly believe God brought us here and I'm very grateful we listened.

We must be willing to let go of the life we planned, so as to have the life that is waiting for us.
Joseph Campbell

_____

_____

_____

_____

_____

_____

_____

_____

_____

_____

_____

_____

_____

_____

_____

Season of Gratitude
Day 30

As November ends, my focus shifts to the message of Christmas – Emmanuel, God with us. He experienced everything we will endure. He understands and promises to be with us through it all. This assurance is the greatest blessing of my life.

The season of gratitude isn't limited to November and Thanksgiving Day. Advent provides an opportunity to continue developing an attitude of gratitude until expressing gratitude becomes a habit.

I pray a special blessing for each reader and journaling friend. As you open your heart this season, may you find the hope, peace, love, and joy Advent and Christmas promises.

The Word became flesh and moved into the neighborhood.
John 1:14 (The Message)

I'm so glad He did. There is indeed something better to come!

The celebration of Advent is possible only to those who are troubled in soul, who know themselves to be poor and imperfect, and who look forward to something greater to come.

Dietrich Bonhoeffer's Christmas Sermons.

_____

_____

_____

_____

_____

_____

_____

_____

_____

_____

_____

_____

_____

_____

_____

_____

_____

Wanda Strange

An Advent Reflection

Last Sunday, something specific about the Advent wreath captivated my attention. Each of four Sundays proceeding Christmas, a family in our church lights a candle representing the preparation of our hearts to celebrate Christ's birth. The first – hope, the second – peace, the third – joy, the fourth – love.

As the candles burned, I noticed the hope candle dwindled. A question persists, "Where do we go when our hope runs low?"

Because we live in a broken world, our hope **will** run low. We experience broken relationships, poor health, financial challenges – fill in the blank with your own endless list of challenges. Feelings of hopelessness and despair rise to the surface. Like the dwindling candle, our hope burns out and runs low.

So, what do I do when my hope is scarce? I focus on Christ, the source of hope. When the prophets despaired, God broke through and sent His Son.

Unlike the candle, which cannot regenerate, our source of hope knows no limits. Christ restores hope, gives peace, joy, and love.

Celebrate this Christmas Season with a grateful heart!

Now the God of hope fill you with all joy and peace in believing, that ye may abound in hope, through the power of the Holy Ghost.

Romans 15:13 KJV

ABOUT THE AUTHOR

A native Texan, Wanda Strange lives with her husband, Kerry, in Bluff Dale, Texas. Married since 1969, they are the parents of an adult daughter, Ginger. Though Wanda retired in 2016, a career in oncology nursing remains her life's work and professional calling. She continues to be actively involved in the local and national Oncology Nurse Society. Her passion for patients and caregivers inspires her to encourage cancer patients, their families, and oncology colleagues. She passionately pursues time with family and friends. Her faith provides motivation to participate in community and church activities. She loves music and books. Faith – Family – Friends comprise the priorities of Wanda's busy life.